Bad Neighborhood

Bad Neighborhood

Poems by

Cindy Frenkel

Cover design by Shay Culligan, incorporating
Marvin Frenkel's portrait of Barbara, his wife
(and the author's mother).
Author photo by Eva Juni

ISBN: 979-8-90146-727-5
Library of Congress Control Number: 2026935817

Kelsay Books
502 South 1040 East, A-119
American Fork, Utah 84003
Kelsaybooks.com

For Marcia Ferstenfeld and Larry,
her husband of blessed memory,
and Barbara Larew-Adams,
and in blessed memory of Forsteen "Tina" Brooks,
without whose love this would not have been possible.

Hannah Maud, you are always the reason.

Acknowledgments

Thank you to Finishing Line Press, especially Leah Maines, Christen Kincaid and their team for publishing my chapbook, *The Plague of the Tender-Hearted;* all 28 poems are included here.

My gratitude to the editors of publications where these and other poems also have appeared, sometimes in different forms:

The Alembic: "Winter Pool" as "Our Winter Pool"
The Art of Days, 2023: "Pointillism"
Divining Dante: "Still, Above Grass"
Insect Dreams (miniature book series): "Ecdysis"
LIBER 3.4: "Vignette"
The Literary Parrot, Series 2: "Slumber and Awakening"
The MacGuffin: "Things I Have to Forget to Fall Asleep," "Lending the Book" as "Miracles," "Edison's Clock," "Goodbye"
Mom Egg Review (MER): "Surrender and Arrival"
The New Yorker: "Pit"
Nu?Detroit: "Coat, House, Watch," "Serving," "Memorial Day, Royal Oak, Michigan," "Questions"
Peacock Journal, an e-zine: "The Anatomy of Color"
Peninsula Poets (Michigan Poetry Society): "Slumber and Awakening," 1st Place, Family Category, "Plate Tectonics," 3rd Place, Margo LaGatutta Memorial Award
Photosynthesis: "August."
Pink Panther Magazine: "Arrival" "And still," "The Last to Leave"
Poetica: "Who'd Notice?" as "Grammatical Choices"

The Poetry Jukebox (and one of 20 poems from the anthology featured in Dublin's Fitzwilliam Square in 2023): "Still, Above Grass"

Poets to Poets: Echoes and Tributes: "In the presence of the marvelous," "Happily We Sit"

PRISM (Lawrence Technological University): "Pointillism," "Through the Criss-Cross Thicket," "Devout Atheist," "Elegy"

Renaissance City Magazine for the Arts (e-zine): "Things I Have to Forget to Fall Asleep," "How You Said Goodbye," "And still," "Facts" as "Imagine It"

Scattered Ecstasies (an exhibition at Sho Art Spirit and Performance in Windsor, Canada): "My Beautiful Solitude," which was one of twenty poems performed by an actor in front of a painting created in response to it.

A myriad of friends have kept me afloat; you know who you are and my thanks are profound. I'm reiterating my gratitude to those acknowledged in *The Plague of the Tender-Hearted,* without naming you all.

Two men, no longer alive, whose belief in me continues to inspire, are Harry Mathews and Galway Kinnell. Much appreciation for my New York literary friends, my childhood and high school ones, my Roeper group, my Sunday morning circle, and the Detroit literary community. Special gratitude to Olga Klekner, Alice Phillips, Ela Harrison, Susan Shapiro, Kathleen Olsen, Karen Klein, Jan Mordenski and the late Maria Costantini.

Two additional poets have been invaluable, Molly Peacock and Mary Jo Firth Gillett. Molly ushered in beloved muses, including Carla Drysdale. Alice Quinn, thank you for your encouragement during these many years and unending gratitude to the late Harriet Walden and the late Don Major. My massive gratitude to the late, great Rabbi Avi Cohen; his validation meant everything.

Rochelle Juni, without your assistance, I could not have finished this on time. Thank you to Kelsay Books, especially Karen Kelsay, Olivia Loftis, and Shay Culligan.

Thanks, too, to my large, loving family, particularly my siblings, as well as Muriel Wetsman Brooks and Nelson Lande. Tom, my late brother, you are remembered. Gratitude to M.G.H., a big, tattooed man, the most eccentric, patient man I know. John Barton, my stellar friend, I could not have made sense of this without your edits.

Contents

When you're alone in your head,
you're in a bad neighborhood.
—Anonymous

Then comes affliction
to awaken the dreamer.
—Søren Kierkegaard

Introduction

It is my great hope that in sharing some of the most painful events of my life that they will be of use and possibly facilitate change in another's familial trajectory. Art can foster compassionate dialogue about addiction and depression, both illnesses whose stigmas need to be addressed. Death by suicide has reached epic proportions in our country, for all age demographics; from children to the elderly, these people don't see any other options. My intent is that this work paints a portrait of a loving family, who sometimes acted out of fear and ignorance, yet never out of malice. To quote therapist Barbara Larew Adams, "If we are complicit in silence, we are complicit with the unintentional transferring of pain."

It is important to mention the phone number 988 for the Suicide and Crisis Lifeline. Another wonderful resource is The Center for Hope and Human Flourishing in Bloomfield Hills, Michigan, run by suicidologist Gigi Columbini. I was fortunate to attend a training with her and Ellen Pare, at Rabbi Daniel B. Syme's urging. Without that information, I would not have known how to appropriately respond to students in crisis, nor could I have written, "In the Classroom." Danny, your friendship and careful reading of this book was invaluable.

I cannot overstate the enormity of constant support from friends and family as I made my way through tumultuous times. My profound thanks to the remarkable people who loved me through, always showing me how beautiful this fleeting gift of life is.

—Cindy Frenkel
May 2026

I.
Keeping Quiet

Serving

in memory of Forsteen "Tina" Brooks

The Fisher Building still bustles
yet in the Sixties, we'd walk
into Himelhoch's, which is now only online,
sells Ethiopian coffee. When I was little,
we'd ride Hudson's elevators, later
have a Maurice salad or go to
Sanders in Royal Oak, which was not
chic yet, for shaved ham sandwiches
and a hot-fudge cream puff. We'd sit on stools
at the counter, my mother and I,
we were always served sitting on those stools—
though not too many years before, down south
the woman I loved among the most
couldn't have sat with us.
I didn't know why then.
Neither did I know most Jews didn't eat
ham sandwiches—we didn't have pork at home—
only crisp bacon, a staple, and never
ever wore a Jewish star around our necks.
Might as well wear an armband
with its yellow-pointed patch.
Those were the days when your pumps
matched your pocketbook,
that's what we carried—not purses—
and ladies lunched, taking small bites
at others, keeping their lipstick clean.
Detroit, booming (how I want it now),
youth, here, with options—

knowing every job has meaning, the need
for plumbers, phone operators, all the valued
salesladies, waiters and counter girls,
salesmen, electricians, mounted police
when cops walked their beats.
I salute all you men and women,
who staffed the elevators,
who showed up over and over,
so we could sit under bright lights
at a clean counter, eating shaved ham.

Letters, 1941

Dear Uncle Meyer,

Thank you for the call.
The interview was Friday—
I was hired on the spot!

The man requested I
fill out personnel papers.
There, I met a different fellow,

filled out their form.
(For religion, of course, I checked "Jewish.")
He looked it over, said *We'll call*

you if we need you—
I'm already hired! I said.
We'll call you if we need you! he repeated.

Love,
Muriel

*

Dear Muriel,

My hands are tied. I'm sorry,
there's nothing more I can do.

Even as G.M.'s treasurer, my hands are tied . . .

Love,
Uncle Meyer

Coat, House, Watch

When The Purple Gang walked
in and shot the deli up,
a bullet nicked my friend's
mother-in-law in the knee.
Her new mink coat,
untouched, drooped
on the chair's back.
Halfway to the hospital,
she insisted on returning,
stepping over bodies
for that coat. When my father
was small, he walked daily
to school. My grandmother
said, *If our neighbors*
offer you a ride,
don't ever get in!
Brutal cold. Snow
storm—the neighbor's chauffeur
lowered the window,
offered little Marv a ride—
No thanks! The cold's
refreshing, he lied. The very
next week, the back of
that house next door blew off . . .

*

In Ukraine, my dad's father
stooped in the attic,
Cossacks below demanding his brother
hand over his heirloom gold watch.
Useless, that watch, as time
stood still, my grandfather crouched,
hearing a cry, thump,
feeling his small space quake.

In the Bath

As a child I collected soaps
from around the world,
found out about the Holocaust
as an adolescent.

Who's in these soaps?
Melt our fat, lather hate,
cleanse world,
bathe in our juices.

My great aunts, the cousins!
What became of them? Ashes, ashes,
those great uncles who believed
they failed to save their families.

Facts

Near war’s end, he began
the impossible death march
from the outskirts of Auschwitz,
one emaciated man carrying his emaciated friend
for nine days, the sheer God luck
of not being shot.

Lending the Book

in memory of Hymie Groskind

When I dropped by your house to lend your wife a book,
the second night of Chanukah, you asked my daughter
to light the menorah. She, only three, held the candle lit
—for anyone else I'd have protested—
but there you were in your short sleeves: 7 7 3 2 3.
I'd never seen your numbers before.
They cattled you well, each European 7 evenly crossed.

Swimming at the Jewish Community Center,
doing laps, I immersed myself in thought,
in my body's soothing repetition until a pretty
lifeguard interrupted to ask, *Are you Orthodox?*
Orthodox! I'd forgotten where I was
or being Jewish. Even here, I couldn't forget.
We're opening the shades, she said.
Soon small boys milled in, wearing yarmulke,
payot—and, suddenly, it was Eastern Europe,
just before the war. Then, I thought of you.

When you returned to Auschwitz with your son,
they charged admission; you shook your head,
held out your arm, and they let you in.
Survivors always travel for a birth or a wedding—
your son's wedding, with your two old friends,
from New Jersey and Philly, the three of you,
together, again, in three consecutive numbers.

Keeping Quiet

When you tell my child, *No, speak softly, ladies don't yell,*
I relive your punishment. I was four years old.
How loud a small body can scream!
To suppress it, impossible.
Before watching TV in the den,
or whatever it was you did,
you locked me in the garage.
I couldn't come in, until
I acted *like a human being.*

Night dark, cement walls cold,
expecting someone to break in, take me,
I pounded on the garage's thick door, yelling
until exhaustion overcame
my body, vocal cords frayed.
Even then, ignored.
Sliding into your Cadillac's back seat,
Mother's station wagon beside,
I breathed in its awful leather newness,
stared at tufted buttons, tried resting without sleep.

Now, I get my daughter out of your home,
I let her scream.
Her beautiful, tiny, perfect self.
I let her scream.

My Daughter and Her Friend Dine with Her Grandfather

All the wine that you can drink, all the steak
you can eat—this is the lap of luxury!

They're underage—a year—I say, *so only one glass, okay?*
My father doesn't get my beef with this.

I drop the obvious, *Addiction runs*
in the family. He looks askance.

What? he asks, as if I'm out of whack.
We have none. Then, I go off.

Just. Like. That. About Tom, shooting up then
shooting a bullet through his head. *Tom's dead!*

I take off, out that dining room, recall
five years back. Tom's breakdown in his childhood

room; his tall frame staring ahead, immobilized
on his bed, tears streaming down his chiseled

cheeks. He broke that pact—silence, stoic
in the land of silent men. I want to cave,

there and then. Tom's sponsor, with another
brother, try to ease him to his feet. He

won’t budge. He’s got to get to the psych ward—
we’ll get him there—to check himself right in.

My Don Juan brother’s broken-hearted.
My father shakes his head, explaining in

an even tone, he *doesn’t understand.*
For years, I tried forgetting what he said

until my father’s shame became my shame, my whole
being wrong: *With how much this will cost,*

you could take a deluxe vacation. And that
was the year I began to disappear.

Who'd Notice?

At first, my mother preferred to say *Took his life.*
I said: *Suicide.*
People thought he overdosed, which made sense:
The exit wound was so high up
an oversized yarmulke covered it, and my family reversed
his casket's direction. (Who'd notice?)
Open casket—
Smartest thing we did, my dying mother said.

No one walked around the backside
where full-blown roses were displayed.

I glanced at him: high cheekbones, sculpted face,
angelic in his white robe, one diamond stud.
I returned to the back room, preparing to perform.

Naturally, my parents rushed home,
brothers, cousins.
An estranged cousin
perused the fine Federal furniture.

The whole city was in the dining room. On the wall
my grandmother's miniatures, verre églomisé silhouettes.
Note the title of the prettiest, *The Happy Family.*
Yes, I know Tolstoy was right, we are not all alike.

One woman asked,
How did he do it? Was he alone?
A man said, *You have his dog?*
Yes, I promised, if anything . . .
So you had a warning, he said. (Who'd notice?)

I woke up, thought Tom wasn't really gone,
descended the steps to my dining room,
saw each shiny black letter engraved
The family of on cream paper.
No one minded I picked out a casket
too ornate. (Who noticed?)
Later, I sent myself away,
repeated, *He put a bullet in his head.*

Goodbye

For months, the dog
in kidney failure.

Thrice weekly, fluid
in his neck's scruff,

incontinence pads near the foot
of my dining table, by the back door.

At night, my students sat at that table—
they came and went, made room

for him to weave about their legs.
One night, Magnet didn't want

to be carried upstairs. Morning,
I came to him. Confused, tangled,

imprisoned in the lamp's cord,
his brown eyes with their white glaze,

asked me, *Please.*
It took thirteen years.

I did not wait.
I took his ashes to my brother's grave.

I opened the bag, turned it
over, and over and over,

I dusted my dog
—Tom's dog—over him.

Elegy

O lost brother in your grave,
I leave my assemblage:
two twigs, a stone. Alone I am
above grass over bone.

Buddy in the Dark

He is never more other than when lights
are out and moonlight's softly seeping in.

Suddenly, he transforms: his eyes flash as
copper coins, reflecting moonlight, powers

alien. Or am I the foreigner?
This was felines' domain millennia

before. Nocturnal, ice-age carnivores,
a Smilodon plunging its saber teeth

to seal the kill. If Buddy had claws to
extend (my rescue cats all robbed of them),

he'd catch his prey, clamp his jaws to crush that
windpipe in, suffocating breath and some-

times song. As with our species, cats are rare;
they'll kill for sport, easy to forget when

he lulls in gentleness. Neanderthals
ate mastodons simply to survive, yet

even now, a domestic cat will go
swiftly for the throat; in merely minutes,

a lifeless body lies. The end game is
the same, as a Kosher butcher's chalaf's

humane cut, while the heart's beating as the
body drains of blood. Is this not still the

way it is, the way it's always been?
Kashrut forbids the mix of meat with milk,

which now seems mostly metaphor, yet still.
Eon of time, compressed, forgotten here,

in my air-conditioned bedroom with its
bead-board trim and blue, antique transferware.

Reclining in my overstuffed chair, book
in hand, content, with three felines

surround sound purr—my tabby and two failed
foster ginger cats, who are well aware

of their success right here. Dropped off one night,
simply nowhere else to go—long, svelte, scared.

Six weeks, at most, I was told, they would stay.
That's right. They arrived, just before the plague!

Yet isn't everything ephemeral,
and we forget to know? Now, Longfellow

tries to scratch the roped post. His claws are gone,
the itch remains. Buddy's tail, an appendage, as a snake,

a slow, wavering dance to tempt Eve, aaah—
it's distraction for any prey to see.

Buddy's riveted by a miniscule arachnid,
upside-down, on the ceiling, a life

I didn't see. Does he want to
clear the room so he can rest atop me,

lose his gaze in mine? Or is he hoping
spiderlings will spill forth up high, scurry

this way and that, a fevered game to ride
the night away? I remove the spider.

Now, his eyes are green, marble-like, each
a planet of oceans vast, each pupil's

glossy landmass contracts. Soon, he's a
miniature lion on my lap, sleek

yet snug, vibrating as a smooth machine.
Q-tip paws stretch towards me, luxuriate

in flexibility, mitten-fingers
open fan-like wide. Endorphins release,

he—we—drift off into an ether space
where together we reside, here yet some-

how non-corporeal. He’s writing his
calligraphic air, then rises in prayer.

Pressing his paw into the softness of
my belly, he shifts weight, alternating

his contentment dance. Now, on his back,
he’s cradled—my lap, primal, maternal.

Surrender and Arrival

Liquid gushing down my thighs
wakes me instantly, 5 a.m.,
trails my path, bed to bath;
phone calls to Dr. Markowitz,
my mother, Tina, the sudden tears.

At the hospital,
Completely transverse,
Markowitz says, rubbing my shoulder,
Emergency cesarean, promises
I'll be fine, has me sign
that my death wouldn't be their fault.
My last moment on earth, in a room
with linoleum tile, fluorescent lights buzzing.
Wheeled to the OR, teeth chattering,
Markowitz with me all the way, hand in mine;
strangers move mechanically
around my nakedness.

Let me know when you begin, I tell Markowitz.
I've already cut into you, he says,
then asks if I want to watch.
Watch? *Yes* I want to, *Yes,*
and the mirror rises like a revelation.

My blood splatters—he lifts the seven red layers
of my belly, slips his hands under my skin
as if reaching into the slit of an envelope.

Tiny birth-wax buttocks, shimmery,
and he turns the small body over,
A daughter! Her first breath!
I'm looking at myself from above,
as they say one does in death.

Raising her is better than

parrot tulips newly drooping in an Aalto vase,
French gardens, English clotted cream,
playing footsie, Botticelli's women at the Uffizi.
Swiss chocolate in Switzerland, Russia's golden domes,
tunnels of the Vatican, lazy days at home.
Endorphin release from exercise,
China's Great Wall, dinner in Bologna.
It's superior to them all.
Hummingbirds up close. Cyrano.
Cold water on a sweltering day. Mozart's concertos.
Taking off stilettos. The scent of lilacs
wafting through the window. Summer's warm breeze.
The relief of a long-awaited sneeze.
A good night's rest, Motown, rainforests, newborn pets.
The Holy Wall in Jerusalem.
Our sweatiest, most loving sex.
Meeting with Gandhi in a private reception.
Long, slow kisses that led to her conception.

Slumber and Awakening

Blue eyes searching, lips latching on,
she wouldn't let go of me until sleep took hold.
Now, nearly grown and hazel-eyed, she studies Latin
in the other room, eats pasta that she's rolled.
She alternates between two beds, two homes,
with the constancy of female friends.

Waving her hands as if conducting the wind,
she talks of boys, first-shaven. Invisible, I drive.
Girls in the backseat, their voices still high and sweetly
soft, overlay each other's phrases in counterpoint.
There must be a goddess I've never read about
who gathers stars only to disperse them.
She opens her palms and stars spill out,
enough to occupy the universe.
The road ahead's so bright it almost hurts.

Three Generations

Roles reversed, everything askew:
my daughter's nine, my mother's seventy-two,
and now they are the exact same weight.
My daughter walks with my mother's gait.

My mother, robed, looks up from her wheelchair
as I brush what's left of her gray hair,
and watch my daughter spoon-feed her ice cream.
Strands of hair are coming down like rain.

They used to sit cross-legged on the floor,
playing "bakery" with candles shaped like tortes,
made brownies for their picnics on the sand—
I watched them in their swimsuits, hand in hand.

Where are you off to? Her first solo drive.
She looks away. *To visit Grammy's grave.*

II.
How You Said Goodbye

Things I Have to Forget to Fall Asleep

Just before evening's end, the list begins:
three piles of laundry, like the mind, divided,
the electric bill, that intrepid old *LIFE*
magazine I've been meaning to . . .
Churchill on the cover,
reminds me of Clementine.
The sad oranges and arugula that need
to be tossed. In New Orleans,
tumbling churches, streets under water.
Another Malaysian airplane missing.
My three cousins
all horribly ill at once,
an outbreak of honesty.
Wondering when our time will be up:
First my mother, then my brother,
slow sinking, rapid fire.
First love, husband, marriage implodes.
A love never to be found again,
still it aches like a mad desire,
the match that can't catch fire.

An Outing of Boating
(or Let's Jump Overboard)

Never mind that the view is exquisite.
This is not what I call a pleasant visit.
We are someplace remote, afloat
on Lake St. Clair in my in-laws' boat.

I thought that all was atypically calm,
but they're ready again to start a storm.
She confides disappointment (she's usually the one)
from months ago at something we'd done.

The wind blows; the sail ripples *rat-a-tat-tat.*
Eating, swaying—that's how we sat.
Two of them and two of us.
Do we have to stay? We must.

There is no place to go: We're completely trapped.
And then the wind steals my expensive hat.

Plate Tectonics

Plates shift, cause and effect—
friction wears against the final straw.
One grinds over the other; less is left.

Marriage dissolves and you reflect
what you sensed (unseen, there really was more).
Plates shift, cause and effect.

No widow's wardrobe yet utterly bereft,
sudden weight loss, you're numb to the core.
One grinds out from under the other; less is left.

You've a daughter to protect.
Gingerly walk: There is no floor!
Plates shift, cause and effect.

For a while you receive a monthly check,
pay the bills, cross out each chore.
One grinds over another; less is left.

And now you start to live beyond the wreck,
home orderly and safer than before;
plates shifted, cause begat effect—
One ground over the other; less is left.

In the Classroom

I mention my brother died by suicide.
The room stops.

In ten years of teaching, I tell them,
I have never said this before.

Yet they lost one student this past fall
so the dean invites me to share

what I wish I couldn't readily recall.
Bringing forth this brother now, and hours later, too,

in another class, on this same industrial carpet,
where long Formica tables stand in rows,

as if order meant reason,
the segue's natural as a river's artery.

There's no rustling of paper. Even the leaves
stop bobbing out the window; the fog lifted seconds ago.

The frames are a still life. In backpack
pockets, cell phones emit waves insensate.

I've introduced them to Septimus Smith
and Virginia Woolf herself,

and Anja Spiegelman, whose photo
they have seen only once—

and know mostly as a mouse. Mental illness
is just that, an illness, and addiction is just that.

For years I took such illness as a personal affront
—depression, addiction—inexorably joined.

Rocks in her pockets. Walk in the water.
Let me know, I say. Ask, I tell them,

when someone's depressed—
ask the question, be specific: *Are you suicidal?*

Remember, *Not Really* is a *Maybe.*
Anything other than a *No* is a *Maybe*

and a *Maybe* is a *Yes.* A *Maybe* is always a *Yes.*

F on the Quiz

for Jan Krist

Q: Why didn't Cinderella's glass slipper disappear at
    midnight?
A: I never had a clue, which bothers me still.

Q: Who said: Money doesn't care who owns it?
A: My brother told it to me, but he's no longer here to ask.

Q: Who wrote the following?
    Daffodils are old-fashioned telephones.
A: Actually, May Swenson used phones as their parallel—
    it took me over forty years to figure that one out.

Q: To whom do you attribute this quote?
    Divorce is amputation by tearing.
A: My friend Jan. She was correct.

Before the Wedding

She wasn't sure, she confessed. Her parents,
nicely dressed, the three seated in the family's library.

She pictures them decades ago with clarity.
There were doubts: she couldn't decide what

was wrong, the flying back and forth or the man himself.
Only the silk dress, ordered not with lace, but handmade

flowers, was perfect. *We'll proceed,* he told
his only daughter. She looked into his eyes.

If you change your mind, even on the very day,
no one will be mad. Her mother interjected,

Marvin! Not the day! Years later, she doesn't miss
her husband much, her father, still, and often totally.

Still, Above Grass
(or Going for a Walk After Reading Dante)

for Franco Costantini

Francesca's memory has one small flaw:
When her affair with Paolo goes astray,
she fails to note he's her brother-in-law.

Study what they did and not what they say.
Just following orders, Eichmann made clear.
Hell's much more crowded since Dante's day.

ARBEIT MACHT FREI—death's taunt austere—
is forged in plain font on the gates of Hell:
Abandon all hope ye who enter here.

The monatto signals his ankle bell,
dragging corpses to graves with hands worked raw,
and air tainted with a rancid-sweet smell.

Drained from the descent through Hell's gaping maw,
I long for earth's light, imperfectly flawed.

Betty's Creek

in Rabun Gap, Georgia

Late day with Jessamine who shows
me trillium's three white petals, spring
ephemeral—as are we—and away

we are on Cove Trail, where the red
crown of a pileated woodpecker's
stark against trees desolate—

an image mediocre as a photograph
glued on pulpy paper I'd ignore in
a small-town gallery I'd make a bee-

line for. A snail emerges from
its shell—still life on bark—inky body
glistening nearly luminescent in the dark.

Shell-shocked, its island
picked up. Our socks and shoes
are off; we dip our feet into cold

mountain water, feel its sting.
Soothing waters above.
Foam laps, little tide, banal,

boring beauty rushing in, rushing out,
layering over water's glossy rocks
sediment threaded with ferny moss.

In, out. Out, in. In, out.
We risk nothing in this dusk.

I am sick of poems

about suicide and artists whose work
is earmarked with it, as if their exits
were major accomplishments.
Why did it ever draw me in?
Parker's clever, rejected options.
Arbus, Rothko, Berryman.
Plath should have baked only bread in the oven;
Sexton's garage door could've unhinged.
Oh, let's not go on with the whole list—

Tom, you put yourself in daunting company.
But that crisp November morning of your funeral,
I walked your nearly feral dog; his nostrils read the breeze.
Collage of wet leaves, rust, gold, green,
littered damp pavement, glistening memento mori.

Still I love

her here, refined, toned, elegant—my father's brush strokes
bring her back again, another oil. She's lounging
on the couch. Now, above *my* couch. She came straight
from my parents' house, around the block,
where in my mind she's forever lying in the library
on the barn-red couch, as she is here, against walls
a mustard-tone—English knotty pine (as are mine).
My father set her in that very room,
then hung her portrait there, above that couch.
Lovely in repose, she's slim, proportional, the languid hand
her head is resting on, her arms, long legs, all outlines
Modigliani-like! Her eyes, blue, soft, open, almond, kind;
her lips, full; the nose, narrow. In her simple steel-gray
shirtwaist dress, her tailored form belies the tacit warmth.

Ever present, though decades gone, her counsel echoes
daily in my mind. Common sense *(Make your bed,*
empty the trash at night), coupled with her wacky wit—
steaming open fortune cookies to insert her own.
Like Rebecca at the well, her empathy endeared
the stranger—strangers whom she spotted at services
on Yom Kippur, a family all alone. She invited
them to break the fast with us. When they arrived
amidst our group—families, neighbors, my parents'
widowed friends—everyone savored fresh food on china
with chrysanthemums, tables set with starched linen,
and fresh, pink, gerbera daisies with their perfect
wheeled-petals, happy flowers within our happy chatter.
Soon that family of strangers became friends, yet that night,
they hadn't a clue that their host, the tall woman
in a tailored suit, had been given only months to live.

Another of His Portraits of Her

My father's precisely got her long swan neck,
clavicles, sleek, chic brown coiffure curved around
her oval face, sharply arched eyebrows,
and her tiny, nose-job nose, where her
nostrils appear straight on, exposed.
My daughter wants this portrait of my mother
I'm hanging here for her. Pop Art/Folk Art recap,
bold Red-White-and-Blue, our flag's the backdrop,
behind my mother's striking head. Look closer:
Those stripes don't align on either side behind,
and in the far-left corner, only three white stars
on navy, descending in a line. She! She's so . . .
contained—redacted, this image of her,
only her head's in view, closeup, restricted, severe,
staring strictly ahead. Frozen in the Seventies,
she's bound by the times, and here she resides:
in this large square where her face appears harsh,
brightly glowing, eyes glaring green, small, nearly mean.

Dahlia's Eyes: Ode to a Shelter Dog

I

Watch how she hates men, and here,
her warning, ears back as she lunges,
revving for a fight, even her eyes threatening
you, you—middle-aged woman, stay the hell
away from the metal fence of my pen!

Barking's shrill, then growling, incessant
refrain echoes off shelter walls.
Let her do this for countless days.

Respond with deep, slow assurances.
Coo, calmly, eyes even at her height.

Coo, lowly, coo.
Listen.

Suddenly—one day—she offers
a cooing in return, faintest hum.

II

Repeat your steady assurance, days.
Next season, just like that,
she will let you walk her,
yet snap unexpectedly—never bite—

in months, you'll acquire
a common language, traversing
Royal Oak's sidewalks,
wet grassy slopes. Inquiring at the base
of a trunk, eagerly she'll inhale
its rough-hewn bark's scent, her nostrils
quivering at rusty, wavy skeletal of leaves,
her path an olfactory symphony you cannot track—
still, she's a distance from you.

III

Enter her pen another day,
retrieve her to meander together—
she neither snaps nor tries to bolt,
instead wriggles her entire being,
her tail madly *thump thump thump*ing
so hard against your shin you
wonder if she'll leave a bruise.

IV

Mild, faint, pale-blue tattoo,
tail's release, affection's epigraph.
Calligraphy in blood's bloom—
who knew it'd please you so?

A year passes, many walks:
She hardly snaps. Wordlessly,
near silence of your breathing,
your body's steady bending,
unhooking the frayed leash,

the wordless dialogue as her paw rises to your hand.
Your eyes meet.
In her shiny irises is trust, her pupils,
lit, wet with gratitude,
then you are thanking her,
stroking the top of her head,
wondering who could harm such a pure being.

V

Later, on a rainy afternoon when you retrieve her,
again you enter the deep caramel puddles of her eyes.
Dahlia, beagle-hound, whose ears graze grass—

when indoors, you want to stay here,
she resting her head in your lap, you sitting in her cage
for hours, indifferent to the shelter staff, who think

you're very, very odd. Stroking her ears' long
velvet flaps, tender in your palm, touching
the cold black contours of her mushroom nose,

you then caress her warm head, its amber spot, as you lean
to the corner of her metal-framed bed
against cinderblock walls, and Dahlia leans into you,
her head on your lap. Interrupting, she lifts her gaze—
your face flooded with Dahlia-kisses.

VI

Two years, your visits' steady ticking, here,
in this no-kill shelter, she waits for you, you her,
and you start to believe she'll always be here,

'til an older couple want her—and you will
have a drawn-out farewell before one day,
you arrive and her cage is empty, you are empty.

VII

In a house nearby you will never see,
you imagine Dahlia as she lifts her right paw
to the woman, and, later—perhaps—even to the man.

Broken Promises

When I was with my mother,
my father made me promise
not to cry. He worried
it would feed her cancer.
I complied. Or tried.

Friday night, shul, my brother
Tom, not gone a month
yet when the rabbi
read his name,
I burst into tears.

Years later, I wondered
if my mother's welled-up grief
grew alongside her cancer
—fluid filling her lungs,
her belly distended, as though

in her seventies, she were pregnant.
She was carrying the grief
of him—her third son—
grief my father mistakenly
forbade her to let show.

Love in Action

My father keeps his secret: her oncologist
confided *six* weeks, holds it in, as though

he'd never heard, while her belly swells.
Peritoneal mesothelioma: what a death sentence.

Googling, we discover it's spreading
in a thin layer of film. He's silent, still,

after Tom's death. Once she outlives
her youngest son a year, he tells us.

Bad Neighborhood

VI–VIII

Stars sprinkle like salt.
The dog goes in and out.

IV

Thrice-trashed,
I kept going back,

wanting to make that childhood right.
My second mother, Tina, on the bright

green grassy lawn, teary with dew.
If I could freeze the picture, I wouldn't feel such pain—

and I'd hear your voice joking—
with a nickname for everyone.

VIII

It took me eighteen years to publish:
Shame was an accessory to your death

as was your gun. Your exit wound
was the final way you left—

the needle did its number,
but we performed the larger theft.

I–X

Parts of Michigan are vast, desolate—
farmland for miles, silos near carpets of grain,
trapezoids of cows, their black spots
whole countries on a map.

III

Father's business went under years before.
Advance Glove Manufacturing Company,

on West Lafayette Boulevard,
the iconic painting of a colossal

terry cloth glove wrapped around
its corner (my father's idea), that very building

now holding books like this.
Look good, look good—

take out the trash. Let in the cat.
May I have directions please?

V

After my mother's cancer,
sickness pummeled in;

we couldn't see before us,
blood-garnet blurred the way—

traffic lights dangled as earrings,
emeralds fulgent in rain.

Trees bent as if pleading.
Lights directing: *Come, Go,*

and love was a cat
arching against a leg, leaning into loss.

VIII

I inherited a showy necklace,
gowns of beaded silk—
all I'd wanted
was to be held when I was five pounds,
drink my mother's milk.
(Five pounds, so small!
Don't touch—she's fragile in the glass.)

V

Our mother had six months
to live, they said. You, thirteen years

clean—you blamed our mother's
cancer for your relapse.

Chemo in her veins, heroin in yours.
We couldn't see your disease dire as hers—

findings might confirm our failings, so ignore.
We gathered round the matron, elegant,

awed by her grace—
yet I pleaded for help for you,

my voice again dismissed—
the only girl, the poet! *(What a waste!)*

I said how sick you were—
Shut up! They shook their heads at me.

II

See the photo on the wall?
Our mother in her maroon velvet gown,
fox shawl, our father in his tux—
They're in their evening wear.

Money covers up a lot
when it's there.

I –

The Nazis didn't have an epiphany—
they just got interrupted.

VI

I cannot . . . it.

V

Our father thought
you were sleeping upright
on the couch—
went closer,
rigor mortis had set in—

I screamed. Pay phone, gas station,
on Woodward Avenue, in a different state
and in a different state,
grateful to have called the cops
to meet them at your door—

I–X

Petrichor, and the fern sprouts;
spiny, spindled shadows
of sage leaves, overflow,
waterfall of tiny, chartreuse lines.
In morning's light, one stem's shadow flits
onto my open palm, dappled sun rains down.

VI

I admit surprise
you discussed his death,
planned to bury him—

VIII

I do not wear my wedding ring;
I wear my mother's wedding ring.
My father's withering.

I wear his wedding ring.
(I show him this.)
He doesn't know what day it is.

IX

Mary Shelley read at her mother's grave,
made rubbings with the letters,
as if naming is saying and saying is sense.

Galway wrote of the Shelleys,
the lie, the myth, and love
is never free—

and a prayer is only a thought.
I want to send up those loving prayers
and declare *yes* today

because I was anchored in the living, dying.
Seven years I was anchored in the sinking.
Living is always dying.

Now, I follow a winding path.
I, the one who could never read a map.

V

Tom's couch was soaked.
A gun went off.

The Last to Leave

While disappearing from her body,
my mother stayed in her condo,
her fragile presence evaporating;
skin outlining bone after bone,
heart's small pulsing
through what was left of her breast,
up-down, up-down breath.

My mother was departing
from the feet up—
mornings, we'd peel the sheet,
the hospice nurse and I,
from her cold, blue-mottled legs.
Hearing the last to leave—

Tom is on the other side,
I whispered, bending over,
stroking her hair, those brief,
longest days of my monologues—
and her parents were there,
her sister, her cousin Bob,
his sister with the dour expression,
whose name I forgot, she knew,

and I knew it was lights out
in the big, beautiful city
I once lived in, my winding streets her veins.
She finally went completely still
and then I slid open the balcony door
so her soul could fly away.

My Daughter's Question

Her grandmother's long dead.
My daughter asks my father
if he could dine with anyone,
dead or living, who would it be?

She expects his answer—
Einstein, Washington or Rembrandt,
his favorite three.
My wife, he responds, instantly.

My Father Insists on Meat Again

His oven is broken, sparse cupboard, no spices;
I slice the meat thin, pour grape-seed oil,
onion soup mix, toss pepper in. Sautéing mushrooms,
sizzling oil, I watch them shrink and my father is shrinking
too, forgets conversing with my daughter an hour ago.

He's in the bed where my mother died,
sleeping away the day. Shades drawn, ratty fabric's
dotted with holes, starlight slipping through.
The ocean's on the other side, dusk seeps
into scalloped empty spaces by the curtain rods,
fabric's fallen from its hooks.

He has swum a half hour—busy day!—today.
When his girlfriend isn't visiting, he wants to curl up
with his aide. We tell ourselves *This isn't him.*

I smash new potatoes—red, white,
dress radicchio, romaine. *Toss! Toss!*
For the fifth time, I insist he rise from bed—
and here he appears: my father!

My father, in his blue bathrobe.
This is the man who tutored me in math,
who bent the fish spine at the dinner table
marveling at its elegance. Here is the man
who wore his beret at the Jeu de Paume,
sketching in his little pad his impression
of Impressionists as onlookers looked on.

The table's set. I present his plate.
He reads my menu's curly script, then laughs:
Frenkel's Impromptu Boeuf avec Chanterelles.
We bite in—tender meat dissolves
on tongues, potatoes smooth and warm. *Delicious!* he says.
Prone to quoting *Iolanthe* these days, he begins:

I wouldn't say a word that could be reckoned as injurious.
But to find a mother younger than her son is very curious.

We smile. He nods.

The Condo

In my parents' room,
I slide next to my father
in the hospital bed, wedged in,
kiss his thin-haired head,
hold his tanned hand, delicate,
blackened from bruising. The bed's
angle replicates my mother's deathbed
years ago. Oxygen tube's even flow,
face flush, feet warm and now
we are pure love—his criticism evaporated
long ago. I, privileged, grateful
he's waited, I'll never be ready
and say things for him alone. Gently
I rise as his aide enters.
He likes them young, pretty.
We speak of nothing significant
unaware he has left, just like that.
As is our custom to let the soul
join its maker, again, I usher
the way, slide open that balcony door.

Is it safe?

My father asked us if the Civil War was over
and could we go outside? *Yes,* we said,
as he sat in his massive recliner in front
of his wide-screen TV, with its tropical film
of birds in their jungle colors flying in front of us.

How You Said Goodbye

Tom, I couldn't get into
the skin you so desperately
wanted to crawl out of
            even though we began in the same womb
not two years apart.

I didn't foresee
what appears transparent
now—those last months—
             your hints
and apologies.

I yearn to go back
to the illusion that
our family's intact,
to have your wide wrist wear this
big Cartier watch,

for you to be dressed
in these sweaters now stacked
in cedar against the moths.
              Simply to hear your voice again
on the phone, your tone rising, past
effusive, brimming with affection:

                                    ter!
Sweet   Sis-
          Sis-

Sweet
                                teeeer!

(Being present with emotion was a punitive condition.)
There you were repeating, with tender candor,

I love you, Cin.   *I love you, Cin.*   *I love you, Cin.*

I didn't recognize goodbye.

Our Winter Pool

I remember my father and me
running out his studio door in bathing suits,
steam rising. He went first, and then
we both went under. A few minutes treading water,
and then we lay, heads pillowed,
side by side on covered mats.
We talked quietly, breath haloed
beneath a canopy of trees—pines'
white boughs bowing in moonlight,
sugar maples dredged in snow—
curved lines frosting
the blue-white night softly coated,
stars dotting sky.
We dipped our heads under
so our hair wouldn't bead with ice.
We spoke now and then, mostly watched.
I ran and he followed, back into the studio;
we slipped on terrycloth robes.
Upstairs, when I fell asleep
my day slipped easily away,
and night was everything I wanted.

Question

I asked a kind man steeped in religion if he knew
the Jewish view on money. *More of it?* he joked,
not meaning to offend. It stung. *Who is rich?*
our rabbis ask. *He who is happy with what he has.*

I thought of *Dallas, Lifestyles of the Rich and Famous,*
our country's chronic coveting, then of the Taj Mahal.
The slaves, we forget, encrusting it in jewels.
The pyramids. And what of them?

A convert taught me my religion's views—money,
a blessing, if come by honestly then shared with others,
something that I wished I'd known. The poor, required still,
to help those less fortunate, unless one is too poor to give.

No shame in that yet not a good way to live. Tikkun Olam!
Repair the world. Leave it better than I found it. When I meet
my maker, will I answer, *Have you welcomed every permitted*
pleasure? I warm my bath and now I step in.

Pit

The peach was
apricot in color—

the fibre wet
beneath its skin,

which held it in.
I consumed the

juicy flesh,
sweet meat meant

to nourish the pit
surrounding it.

A miniature sunset:
burnished hazy red,

within its bleeding
hues, there lodged

the stone, undulated
as a brain, dormant

yet alive. Reposed
within orange-and-apricot,

its seed within that stone—
harboring cyanide, just enough

to keep the deer at bay—
it could have procreated, this

pit-then-seed. And part
is now a part of me.

Memorial Day, Royal Oak, Michigan

I bought fresh tulips, which I was once told
was forbidden in Nazi Germany,

then brought them home: white pitcher with yellow
blooms striated pink, green arches droop

their acrobatics jauntily. In my straw
hat, I stroll on the sidewalk, move freely

towards my friends at the soft-serve stand, where
our hair's blowing in the wind—mine, white, one friend's

black corkscrew curls, the other's straight and blonde.
Silent, grateful, no need for ID

on my sleeve—my mother admonishes
still, *You don't want to live in Royal Oak!,*

Father Coughlin's words in her head.
She's long dead. Yet here she lives. We support

the veteran, who trades paper poppies
in exchange. Sitting on a bench, the dense

shadows interrupt our light: three sprightly
forms mimic us, though it's only we who

recognize our great good fortune now,
on this, an otherwise ordinary day.

III.
The Sky’s Red

Vignette

Since Harold's partner died first,
I'm gifted his antique Flow Blue teapot,
sugar, creamer, which I keep
next to the porcelain pitcher where
my father's wooden paintbrushes show
their bristles like little bud-brooms.
These sit atop a thick, large navy splatter-
ware plate I threw at Bennington
more than forty years ago.

What remains? I recall the feel of wet clay,
sitting at the wheel, centering myself.

Pointillism

in memory of Robert Steele

I'm a passenger riding a fast train,
the landscapes blend and appear the same.
I can only recall a blur of green,
trying to decipher what I have seen.

People, too, capture such spots in my mind.
I remember them, moments stopped in time:
Their eyes, her dress—even a simple hat—
thoughts connect, and perception is just that.

Devout Atheist

Faith is invisible, I say
to your reply, *No empirical data!*

Absurd! Like saying the sky's red.
Sometimes it is, I say.

The Anatomy of Color

I

Green yields itself to us
this time of year,
the hopeless birch, felicitous willow,
and even the pink tulips,
with their green stands and leaves,
bend over as most any flower would
in such a breeze. Air rushes in
with the smell of green, tries to articulate
the pure cerulean of the sky
and fails. But somehow the sweet
smell lingers, and the willow
mops the sky. Through the miniature gray boxes
of the screen door I can see: two red metal
chairs with their fanned backs,
a yellowish straw mat to wipe one's feet on,
and the lawn's vast expanse,
a variety of greens—mint, army, pine.

The paper with its black-on-white
characters is tossed near the door;
its scroll shape rolls, morning
after morning, just beyond the green.
Incarnadine, slender fingers push open the door.
Coffee's smell wafts
through this small house,
and look: the table's ready, the white
porcelain cup reflecting the silver
of a fork, *sizzle* then *splatter*
of breakfast cooking.

Doesn't the sky seem bluer today?
The colors outside more
of what they are, each piece of fruit,
every dirty lawn chair, each blade of hair.
Even the air carries the smell of color:
apple blossoms' explosion, pink and white.
Brushing a mosquito away from the face,
feeling that calm at seeing lawn,
gray-brown bark of a tree,
violet in a bud, *green,* green again,
green as only summer, in a stem.

II

Night is the darkest blue punctuated
by white dots. Iridescent blue wings flutter
between brown trees, and individual nouns
are trying to spell *Forever.*
Color and form divide, distinguish,
modify, as everything ages.

The moon is only a chip of gold, a transmutation
of its old substance, adequate light
to catch the lilacs bobbing. The elm
in the back of the house has been standing
for hundreds of years, the blue wings
flickering for maybe a moment.

Marianne Moore's Hat-Box

. . . or quite the opposite—the old thing, the medieval decorated hat-box, in which there are hounds with waists diminishing like the waist of the hour-glass, / and deer and birds and seated people;
—When I Buy Pictures

When the old man took only my image,
my soul leapt away.
It is most uncomfortable, no surprise,
not to move my body.
Exceptionally awkward are the deer next to me;
any human with half a brain can see
I have never met these deer,
and they have never seen me.
We are at standstill, but the birds
(pheasants, which my whelp mate would adore,
as he's quite the hunter),
I'm sure will be chattered about,
for spreading their rusty feathers in midair,
or, if nothing else, should make a fine main course
with cranberries and rice.
Those people in simple clothes,
and constant nagging smiles.
They look more posed, more insecure,
obsessed, almost, at how they appear.
I cannot scent where their souls are.

Arrival

You are a watercolor in the distance,
a fleck of green against gray,
a Chinese landscape.

You stand in the gazebo.
The gazebo's poles are brushstrokes;
you are blurry in fog.

Morning arrives. A willow interrupts
the red disk. Your brown boots
disturb the dewy grass.

This has been

my biggest surprise.
Large, tattooed man,
shaved head, hoop in ear,
love in air, old-
fashioned protector.
Factory worker, defender.
He invites me for hors d'oeuvres.
Camille Saint-Saëns, Jay Ungar, Annie Lennox,
he likes them equally,
as well as felling trees.
He shoots straight, eats his quarry,
donates what he can't.
He presents me with a rolled
khaki sheet; it's the only paper
from his home long enough to protect the gift
he's grown. Unfurling reveals a human
target, complete with scoring rings,
cradling one red, massive, long-stemmed rose.

Just a Moment

When I called, impromptu, to drive over to
the clean, ordered home of the tall, bald man,
he sounded surprised yet said come on by,
then tried to kiss me as he let me in.

First I need to quickly pee, I explained.
By the sink, I looked down at the floor where
where one long chestnut tendril rested . . .
My mind went wild. *Idiot!* I thought,

my radar's broken. *How did I fall for that mask*
I know, disguising itself on a different man's face?
Water soothed as I washed. I stared at my reflection,
stepped back, looked down. Suddenly compassion

joined me and we erupted laughing; upon closer look at that
lone, long strand, it was *my* hair, curly, just resting there.

Dusk Love

Sky darkens, night settles in,
and I crave your soft skin,
yeoman's muscles,
warmth of arms, biceps' light hair,
the rise and fall of your chest,
its keloid scar-stripe down the center.

This, Love, is the plague of the tender-
hearted, the very limits of it all—
I remember the surgeon
saying men like you would be tender longer,
barrel-chested, big guys.
After they moved you
from intensive care
you began to relax,
until your heart raced,
the alarm sounded,
a machine bleating
Do Not Resuscitate
repeating its death knell;
the staff swarmed
around you, and you
spoke of your father's death.
They shooed me away.
You wanted water.

Walking with the nurse
to the kitchen, opening the freezer,
I held my head in, fanned my watery eyes,
filled your cup, returned with arms outstretched.

The staff busy around you still,
speaking in their foreign language.
Later, when it was calm again, you moved
into silence.
I tried to read, but looked up,
kept looking up,
at your beautiful, flushed face,
high cheekbones,
small, straight nose,
ombré gray goatee,
wild Russian eyebrows,
wires all in the right order,
the whole of you, the absolute whole.

August

Wind thread around the hook's shank,
tie in two biots for its tail, then wrap the fur.
Now, add wings. Your blue-winged olive mayfly's
ready now. A day later, wearing chest waders,
you stand in clear water, on ancient stones polished by
water's flow. Pine scents the wind. Over your shoulder,
your line loops on air—you cast the fly, lands on water.
The trout rises, misses it. You'd release him anyway . . .

Branches like antlers float past.
Night deepens, azure against silhouettes of trees.
The moon's mirrored on water, shimmering.

Edison's Clock

That clock on the mantle in your Fort Myer's lab
echoes your sentiment. Two thin, round
slices of wood—larger, face, smaller, pendulum—
reveal concentric lines, nature's way of marking time:
the clock's devoid of numbers, hands.
You, with your filthy hands,
often misconstrued as the boiler mechanic,
knew what counted wasn't the length one toiled,
only the discovery. You cleaned up well
that snowy, December night,
all decked out with the swells from New York,
your audience far exceeding Mrs. Astor's 400,
who came west to Menlo Park for the theatre of light.
The set, not extravagant—merely farmland—
but your miniature globes of fire
starkly lit the dusty street among the cows and pigs.
Wet dirt glimmered by the boardwalk's planks,
and the trees partook in the windy dance,
white flecks backlit, slowly descending;
the lamplight looked like God's calling,
encompassing all in incandescent light.

733 in the 313

Tonight, the moon's glow—a waxing crescent—
while sunlight illuminates its surface,
is perfect harmony. Not weeks ago,
it appeared as a hemisphere and I
was walking then, as I am walking now,

and we were spinning on our axis, as
we are spinning now, moving three or four
directions all at once. Going around
the sun, nearly seventy thousand miles
an hour, our solar system's orbiting

the Milky Way. At every hour, it's half
a million miles. This makes me dizzy.
Riding your Katana at one eighty,
I thought you were crazy—grateful not to
have known you in those days. Now, I'm riding

The Earth Train near Detroit, travelling at
seven hundred thirty-three. I'll lie down,
your massive TV glowing, unaware,
as are we, that everything is spinning.
There's comfort in you lying by my side

while our galaxy hurtles through this wide,
expanding universe. My resentments,
nursed, are your weighted burdens, an ox yoke:
You refuse to travel . . . but that's a lie.
We're not lying still even though so it seems.

Your logic's inverse. We are travelling,
even the dead. Now, my question is posed:
why bother to wander our small planet
if we are roaming always anyway?

You won't. I seethe. Your suitcase never fills.
At night, you're at the sink, dispensing pills.

Our Different Narratives

for Julie Tirony

Tess is raggedy yet still elegant—
fur tufts tucked between her black padded toes.
Ears turn independently, sonar cones
hone in on subtle cues. She's eloquent

in her moves, gliding stealthily to sound.
At my window, she appears taciturn
while decoding motions I cannot discern,
imagining the stalk and kill on ground.

Above her eyes, her Tabby **M**'s emblazed;
her gaze is fixed below: this dove's assault.
Slowly, her fringed ears turn. Now, it's my fault—
I've call her out, disrupt these ancient ways.

The dove eats, unaware of a failed hunt.
Tess sits. Her tail's a stole, wrapped opulent.

Frida

Everyone keeps painting you with a unibrow.
I don't like it. I want them to paint you
the way you painted it—strong, yes,
with a dip in the middle, a black bird in flight.
I want them to paint you
bedecked and regal, being carried in
your four-poster bed, lifted above
the fray, you, the more loyal of the two,
you, the true survivor, even if your life
was cut short and shorter and heartbreak
did you in, in its way, you still knew
that the world was full of unimaginable possibilities,
which you plumbed—images, floating,
into our minds from above us, like a halo,
like a great big, swooping bird.

There Comes a Time

after Wallace Stevens' A Glass of Water

When you say goodbye to the world,
as I do now: goodbye to the clothes that hid me,
to the armor of silks, linens, and pure wools,
to the city house or country place,
to those friends you don't miss
since they talk about other friends—
signs, on and off the road—the warnings.
There comes a time when you discard
such things, and there is no mourning.

In the weft and weave of new garments,
very old ones, really, you return
to your original self, before the angel
kissed you and left the seal,
before the imprint above your lips,
before your eyes opened and yet you saw
all you needed, before you tested
ripe blueberries with their powdery sheen,
before you observed the silver-filigreed skeleton
of one dried Chinese-lantern pod,
before you inhaled a peony,
or snow's crisp watery scent.

Spanx

I swore, at sixty-three, I'd never wear
those things again. Is there a metaphor
in the name alone? A trademark slap—

to hold me in my place and keep me in?
And. Yet. It did, with an open crotch,
so I could pee without undoing it entirely.

It held my breasts in, too, its straps
shoulder-traps, but my sheer black hose
with the long pencil line that went up

the back of each leg led to a cotton crotch.
I had to cut it out, so openings lined up.
And there I was—all set to go.

Ecdysis

In Indonesia, photographs are shot
of the bright green grasshopper
molting from her ghostly shell,
dangling from a hairy stem.
Emerging from her milky replica
(that sheer, articulated exoskeleton,
luminescent in the sun), she hangs
together with her former sheath, upside down
and side by side, until her newest self is dried.

After Covid, there's fog

invisible. Watching my neighbor's dog,
Miss Maisel, a King Charles Cavalier,
whose ecstasy at seeing me

—she's madly squiggling—
is joy transmissible. I've caught it!
If she could leap out of her form, she would.

She's trapped, strapped, intact.
In fact, she's leaving tracks along with me.
Three weeks in. I'm out! The DNA is clear:

Blake's universe is here. The sycamore drops its bark
in peels of sheets. Maisie sniffs the maple leaves,
head lifts to catch this breeze, underarms of trees;

then her nose a ship's mast pointing straight ahead
and up. Ears flap back. Now, down; acorns
on the ground, their little caps, propellers

scattered in the grass. Massaging her back, she rolls
luxuriant on grass miraculous, reveling
in the now, this elixir we've been waiting

for—and here it is, and here again!, completely
in her field. Isn't my attempt to grasp her reach
precisely what Browning thought a heaven's for?

Five Minutes, Twelve-Years Old

He touched me
this way and that,
my body felt good
but I didn’t want it,
which I said loud and clear—
but not too loud
in case someone
else could hear.
After the waterfall,
I knew, too,
no one would believe
what I went through.

Peers in a Park: A Forgiveness Tale

When I was grown, I saw him once again—
he, with twin daughters and our family friend.
They waved, so I gave my slanted-fake grin.
He was fawning at his daughters, blonde girls

with bangs, wearing smocked dresses, Mary Janes.
Then they walked over and we talked awhile.
I felt warmth I didn't want; he seemed kind.
His twins pulled our friend to the park swing set.

Heart pounding, I brought up that afternoon,
which I thought he'd deny. He, mortified.
Ashamed all this time, he looked in my eyes.
He apologized, again and again.

The past, packed, was always hovering there.
Suddenly, that weight disappeared in air.

Emily D. in the Hood

My small students
have hidden lives
of which they write,
my sole reprieve.

Home is no lovely
clapboard house,
affection blowing in.
Litter scatters with the wind.

Bobby B.'s amber eyes
shine as I recite
I'm nobody! Who are you?
Are you nobody, too?

I've entered with my talking stick,
a man's face carved into it,
and we talk poetry.
Today, everything is Emily.

Do they know where she was raised?
Bobby shoots up his hand,
head tilted, genuine, unhesitant,
asks, *In the hood?*

How could I not make a poem of this?
Emily would be appalled, asbestos
peeking through an opening.
The windows offer up blue-gray

amidst flowers potted on front porches
down the street, bars on every door,
three houses caving in.
On a lawn a couch sits vertical.

No doubt, she'd be dismayed
though note its irony—
graffiti on the overpasses—
their writings on the wall.

Is There a Poem Here?

for Diane DeCillis

At first I felt Buddy kept me amused,
with his head tilted and his stare confused,
one paw swatting black letters on the screen,
intent on catching something he's just seen.

The letters are a flock of birds in flight;
the screen's white glow mimics our midday light.
He tries to catch something that can't be caught.
(Some things, you know, are things that can't be taught.)

Our odd duet: Keys click, he purrs. I grow
annoyed. He blocks my view and ruins my flow.
Not interested in what my writing means—
this also means we rarely disagree.

Letters leap on the screen yet stay in place.
We wonder where things go in ether-space.

In the presence of the marvelous

for Molly Peacock[1]

I'm invisible—and my mouth is zipped.
It's England, the late eighteenth century.
Mary Delany sits in luxury,
alone. I observe her precisely snip
a crisp paper, place it—a ruffled tulip—
on a black background. At her apogee,
she's seventy-two, making history.
Immersed in her world, I'm in the backdrop

of this widow who invents collage.
I notice she cuts a frill of iris, piece
by piece orders her life, lets the paint dry,
gingerly layers bud on vine, each crease
smoothed smartly by her firm hand and honed eye,
life created anew—my own release.

---

[1] *Title excerpted from p. 229 of* The Paper Garden *by Molly Peacock.*

Through the Criss-Cross Thicket

I

Amid the thrum of rain, I lie
sprawled on worn, cotton sheets
side by side with my tuxedo cat; her eyes startle—
one jade green, one sea-blue, of equal hue,
my face reflected in her irises, the black diamonds,
and her pink pads stretch towards me,
that black tail rising, tipped with
a white dot, her exclamation point.
She nestles in, whirring, and there my dreams begin . . .

II

Lost as once in Hastings, East Sussex,
returning solo to my friend's
through the criss-cross thicket late in day,
brushing against brush, spines of thorny branches,
my bearings gone, long shadows,
animal sounds, my heart's thumping
as arms of branches turn ominous
in their clarity. Suddenly, God's reprieve—
a clearing—this open field, its ferny lushness.
Here, clear, sky bright, one blue shade, wide-water view,
panorama of stone buildings dotting around that old castle,
everything spread out like a great quilt.

III

In my old, uneven house,
ordinary loveliness everywhere,
aging oak floor, grains swirling
into darker grains, as when I stir batter,
watch it eddy into itself,
lines in my palms, patterns of a fingerprint—
and music—yes—Bach's flute concerto
in the background, notes gliding, merging
these worlds: cat, white sheets, wood floor,
rain's soothing static, its wavy lines
trickling down window panes.

Domesticity

All day the incessant rain
tap dances on my roof again.

Spring's first downpour.
Outside's a blur.

Trees are massive sponges
soaking it up. Drum-comfort-thrum,

quilt on my lap, I'm ready to take a nap.
Even Earth itself admits change

is coming, confessing in blooms:
How can a garden be where sin begins?

'Splain it to me, Lucy! Spring daze.
Color shouts its adolescent phase.

Five mornings in a row, three petite purple-and-yellow
irises stand perfectly upright on my sill, delighting me still.

My Beautiful Solitude

Remind me what I'd tell
my younger self?

First, feel your feelings:
Don't be afraid of pain.
Know you will walk through it.

Then, call your closest friend again.
For now, you're safe.
Let that sink in.

And you've the tools
to handle trouble
should it come.

Time's tincture is
what you need—
and morning's here.

Look: the sun!
The dappled trees, their long shadows—
resting figures—on the grass.

The cat explores my knees.
Good things will come to pass.

Sssh, Don't Tell

When I opened my mouth, the truth popped out—
so I stuffed it down with flour, sugar, and wheat.
After all, a girl has to eat—and how to act sweet
when anger's brewing? I know how to be: Be angry at me.

Yet, in this place, truth and kindness stroll,
without malice or gossip. Fellow Travelers,
there is unfettered gratitude when you open your arms,
ushering me to safety, where truth isn't a curse

and peace is forged through words, turning
bruises to balm. This magic I cannot fathom.
Words mingling, sentences rising as the sun,
hovering mid-air, light rising, white and clear.

Happily We Sit

We sip wine, companionably, watch bees hover
into foxglove's spotted trumpets and larkspur while cats
curl in circles beneath ferns cascading from terracotta pots.
You're the most indecisive person I've ever known,
you admonish. I instantly reply, *I'm not sure that's true!*
We laugh. You pinch a dead hydrangea head.
We lower our faces, take tipsy selfies,
document our newly doubled chins.
Larkspur. Phlox. I sense scents: Lavender stocks abloom.
Above ground you've spun word-worlds,
planted in soil among roots of elms.
Mirroring the ombré sky, pearl-white petals
of evening primrose open slowly, slowly close.

And still,

when you step out
of your own door
every morning the crisp air stings
with kisses, laughter erupts like a wild stream—
you never dreamt you would find
your deepest love alone.

About the Author

Cindy Frenkel's poetry appears in publications ranging from *LIBER* to *The New Yorker,* as well as in anthologies. Her chapbook, presciently titled *The Plague of the Tender-Hearted,* was released during Covid from Finishing Line Press. Among the places her prose appeared are *Vanity Fair, WIRED.com,* and *The New York Observer,* where she was a columnist. A Hambidge fellow, Frenkel earned her MFA from Columbia University. She's taught literature and writing from elementary school through college. Frenkel served as a writer-in-residence with InsideOut Literary Arts Project, which brings working poets into city schools. Her essay "Sharing Voices, Acting Crazy" appeared in their anthology *To Light a Fire*. "Galway Kinnell and the Blue Button-Down" was in *The Southampton Review*. "15 lessons from 9 years of teaching" was printed overseas in *WRITERS IN EDUCATION.* Frenkel edited the *Detroit Institute of Arts* magazine and co-authored *100 Essential Books for Jewish Readers* with Rabbi Daniel B. Syme.

For more, please visit:
www.cindyfrenkel.com

www.ingramcontent.com/pod-product-compliance
Lightning Source LLC
LaVergne TN
LVHW090614110826
845146LV00001B/383